G

POCK

HARDY
PERENNIALS

ndi Clevely

635.932

Author Biography

Andi Clevely has been a working gardener for nearly thirty years. He began his career in Leeds City Council central nurseries and since then has worked in many gardens around the country, including Windsor Great Park. He is now responsible for a country estate and large garden in Stratford-on-Avon where he lives with his family. Andi has written a number of gardening books and presents a weekly gardening programme.

Acknowledgements

The publishers would like to thank Loseley Park and Gardens, Guildford, Surrey; The Royal Horticultural Society Gardens, Wisley, Surrey; Savill Garden, Windsor Great Park, Berkshire; Rumsey Nursery and Gardens, Clanfield, Hampshire, and Mrs Harriet Jones, Thatcham, Berkshire. All photographs © BBC (Jo Whitworth).

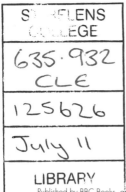

Published by BBC Books, an imprint of BBC Worldwide Limited,
Woodlands, 80 Wood Lane, London W12 0TT

First published 1998
© BBC Worldwide Limited 1998
The moral right of the author has been asserted

ISBN 0 563 38419 0

Artwork by Pond and Giles

Set in Futura

Printed and bound in Belgium by Proost NV
Colour separations by Radstock Reproductions Limited, Midsomer Norton, Avon
Cover printed in Belgium by Proost NV

Common Names

INTRODUCTION

Hardy, herbaceous or border perennials, as they are variously known, are the mainstay of most gardens. They make up a huge diverse group of dependable species which flower at a given season each year, most of them dying down in autumn and reviving in spring. 'Perennial' is a relative quality, and plants may live for just a few seasons or, in the case of peonies for example, for half a century. All gradually increase in size, however, and propagating them every so often will rejuvenate them.

Planning with perennials

There are perennials for every situation in the garden, and the main difficulty is selecting from the enormous range available. The first priority is to assess where they are to grow and to make sure your chosen plants will be happy there. All varieties have cultural preferences, whether for cool shade or a sunny dry bed, and different habits – there are dwarf, slow-growing varieties for edges or small borders, and tall vigorous kinds that need plenty of room.

Design is a matter for personal taste, but as a general rule a border against a fence or wall is best planted with tall varieties at the back, behind progressively shorter species, so that all can be seen clearly. Or position tall kinds in the centre of island beds viewed from each side. Some choice plants are effective as single specimens among other kinds, but many are best planted in threes, or larger groups, to make a strong impact and avoid looking fussy.

It is often a good idea to choose plants in flower – colours and shapes vary subtly, and it is important that you like them and that they blend comfortably with neighbouring varieties. Although a few perennials (Crambe cordifolia, for example) are single species, most have dozens or even hundreds of different forms, and this book can offer only a taste of the cornucopia available.

Preparing the ground

Adequate soil preparation before planting essential. As the entries indicate, some plants like to be grown in deeply dug ground, whereas for others you need only loosen the soil by forking. Try to remove all weeds, including root fragments of perennial weeds, and then improve the soil according to its type and the plant's needs.

Heavy soils: Many of the stronger perennials enjoy soil with plenty of body, but if there is a danger of waterlogging in winter dig in plenty of grit or fine gravel where recommended, to open up the structure and assist drainage. Keeping the surface covered with a coarse mulching material such as bark helps to prevent the surface from becoming greasy after rain or from cracking in dry weather.

Light soils: These normally drain freely, and it is often necessary to add moisture-retentiv organic material such as garden compost, leaf mould, composted bark or decayed manure so that roots do not dry out too fast in summer. Nutrients also leach quickly during rainfall, so add plenty of organic matter, before planting and as mulches, and feed plants regularly.

Planting perennials

Plants bought in containers may be planted whenever the ground is not frozen or too wet, but there are optimum times when plants settle in without the need for much attention. Autumn is ideal for most species, while spring is the best alternative – and is

metimes preferable on heavy ground that
ght be wet and cold in winter.
The same simple planting procedure
plies to most species.

Cultivate the site thoroughly beforehand,
preferably a few weeks earlier, and add
organic material or grit as recommended
in the text. Always prepare an area at
least twice the size of the plant's rootball.

Arrange a collection of plants on the
surface. Then dig out a hole for each,
large enough to take the roots without
cramping them and at the same depth as
the plant was growing. Break up the
excavated soil and mix in any fertilizer.

Soak the plant for a few hours, drain and
then remove from its container. Stand it in
place, backfill around the roots with loose
soil, and firm gently.

Water in well if planted during dry
weather, mulch where recommended.
Don't forget to label the plant for future
reference.

are

eding: Annual feeding, usually at the start
the season, is important to fuel new
owth; sometimes further feeds are
visable during the season. Unless
ggested otherwise, a general balanced
anular or powdered fertilizer is best;
uid feeds can be used for supplementary
plications. A nutritious mulch of very
od compost or decayed manure is an
ceptable substitute.

atering: Requirements differ widely, and
er-watering varieties that like dry soil can
e as lethal as neglecting moisture-loving
nds. An occasional thorough soak is more
eful than frequent light sprinkles; evening
the best time, when evaporation is minimal
d water can percolate to the roots.

Support: Tall varieties often need support to
prevent their sprawling across neighbouring
plants. A range of proprietary stakes is
available, or you can often use twiggy tree
branches or peasticks. Alternatively, grow
shorter sturdy varieties in positions that are
exposed.

Pruning: Most perennials die down each
autumn, so there is no woody growth to
prune, but they often need cutting down
when tidying beds at the end of each
season. Deadheading flowers and cutting
back between flushes of bloom can be
important, and many tall varieties may be
shortened by half in early growth to keep
them compact.

Propagation: The main clump or crown of
a perennial normally expands each year,
sometimes dying in the centre or becoming
so crowded that flowering declines. Before
this happens, plants should be renewed,
usually by division: dig up the plant and
split it into smaller pieces with a spade, or
with two digging forks pressed back to
back to lever it apart. Always replant
younger outer portions. Alternatively, pieces
can be chopped off with a spade in situ
without disturbing the main clump, or
cuttings may be taken.

It is also possible to raise many perennial
species from seed.

And finally ...

Hardy perennials are the easiest plants to
grow, but they may not all succeed equally
well. Some may languish because the site is
unsuitable or they are not quite hardy
enough for your district. Try them
somewhere else in the garden, or
experiment with some of the other varieties
from the huge and exciting range that is
available. And remember to grow plenty for
indoor flower arrangements.

ACANTHUS SPINOSUS

Acanthus is an easy-going plant, except where its roots lie in wet soil in winter, and very sturdy – its flowering stems often reach a great height without the need for support. When cut, the flowers last for many weeks in water. Grow plants as a bold specimen clump where the architectural foliage will make the maximum impact.

Flowering time: Mid-summer to early autumn.

Height: 90cm–1.2m (3–4ft); flowers up to 1.8m (6ft).

Spread: 90cm (3ft).

Soil: Any except poorly drained clay.

Positioning: Full sun or light shade; 45–60cm (18–24in) apart in mid-border; in a warm position with plenty of room.

Care: Plant in autumn or spring in well-dug soil with plenty of compost. Feed in spring with general fertilizer, mulch light soils with compost. Protect young growth from slugs. Deadhead. Cut down top growth in mid-autumn. Chop back invasive roots in spring and summer.

Propagation: Divide in early autumn or spring; sow in a frame in spring.

Recommended: Basic species and Spinosissimus Group (silver leaves).

Useful tip: In heavy soil bed plants in sharp sand or grit.

Related plants: A. mollis, variegated 'Holland's Gold', Latifolius Group.

Achillea millefolium Milfoil, Yarrow

Flowering time: Early to late summer, again in mid-autumn.

Height: 30cm–1.2m (1–4ft).

Spread: 30–60cm (1–2ft).

Soil: Any well-drained soil.

Positioning: Full sun, some shelter from strong winds; 30–45cm (12–18in) apart in groups of 3 in mid-border or as background.

Care: Plant in spring in well-dug soil with added bonemeal. Feed in mid-spring with a general fertilizer. Support taller varieties in exposed sites. Trim back after flowering; cut down all growth in late autumn.

Propagation: Divide in spring or autumn; sow outdoors in late spring.

Recommended: Basic species and fine varieties like 'Cerise Queen', 'Lilac Beauty'.

Useful tip: The dry brown seedheads are popular for flower arranging.

Related plants: A. filipendulina and 'Cloth of Gold', 'Gold Plate'; A. ageratum, white 'W. B. Child'; dwarf A. umbellata; also hybrids like A. 'Fanal', 'Moonshine'.

ACHILLEA MILLEFOLIUM

The many fine white and richly coloured hybrids of this long-flowering perennial, once a plain pungent herb and weed of lawns, are particularly happy on dry soils. All forms have attractive ferny leaves that have sometimes been used as a salad herb. Choose varieties with care, as heights vary widely.

AGAPANTHUS 'LOCH HOPE'

All shades of blue, from rich navy to the merest hint of colour, are represented in the numerous hybrids of this elegant South African member of the lily family. The species are less hardy than hybrids but all kinds can be grown against a warm wall, where the tall slender flower spikes will lean gracefully towards the sun. Plants resent disturbance, so do not move them unless absolutely necessary.

Flowering time:	Mid-summer to early autumn.
Height:	60–90cm (2–3ft).
Spread:	38–45cm (15–18in).
Soil:	Moist, well-drained.
Positioning:	Full sun or very light shade, in a warm sheltered site; 30–38cm (12–15in) apart in groups of 3 in mid-border, against walls and in containers.
Care:	Plant in autumn or spring, 5–8cm (2–3in) deep in well-dug soil with plenty of compost or decayed manure. Water when dry in spring and summer. Deadhead. Cut down in autumn, cover crowns with manure or compost.
Propagation:	Divide roots in spring; sow in a frame in spring.
Recommended:	'Headbourne Hybrids' also 'Ben Hope', 'Loch Hope', 'Peter Pan', 'Tinkerbell'.
Useful tip:	In cold gardens, grow in tubs or half-barrels and insulate from frost.
Related plants:	*A. campanulatus* (hardiest), including white var. *albidus*, 'Isis', ssp. *patens*.

Flowering time: Early and mid-summer, sometimes later.

Height: 30–45cm (12–18in).

Spread: 60cm (24in).

Soil: Moist, with good drainage.

Positioning: Full sun or semi-shade; 30cm (12in) apart as ground cover under shrubs, edging to borders.

Care: Plant in autumn or spring in well-dug soil with plenty of compost. Feed in spring with general fertilizer, mulch with compost. Water in dry weather. Support lax growth with twiggy sticks. Deadhead before seeds are ripe to prevent self-seeding.

Propagation: Divide in autumn or spring; sow in a frame in spring; transplant self-sown seedlings.

Recommended: Basic species and large-flowered 'Grandiflora', 'Robusta'.

Useful tip: The most luxuriant foliage develops in moist dappled shade.

Related plants: *A. conjuncta* and *A. alpina*, rockeries; *A. erythropoda*, neat and compact.

ALCHEMILLA MOLLIS

Alchemilla is an easy-going cottage garden plant, undemanding and welcome in any planting scheme. Its fluffy branching sprays of tiny flowers and pleated grey-green foliage are both popular for cutting; the leaves are as soft as suede and are covered in fine hairs that trap drops of rain and dew.

Anemone × hybrida Japanese Anemone

ANEMONE × HYBRIDA 'GEANTE DES BLANCHES'

These valuable late-flowering perennials are vigorous and majestic in a border, but equally at home in a wild garden where the tall graceful stems hold the numerous bright 5cm (2in) blooms clear of surrounding grasses and flowers. Plants take time to establish, but then multiply gradually into large satisfying clumps.

Flowering time:	Late summer to mid-autumn.
Height:	45cm–1.2m (18in–4ft)
Spread:	45–60cm (18–24in).
Soil:	Any fertile soil.
Positioning:	Full sun or light shade, sheltered from strong winds; singly or 45cm (18in) apart in groups of 3, in woodland gardens, middle of borders.
Care:	Plant in autumn or spring in deeply dug soil with plenty of compost or decayed manure. Feed with general fertilizer in spring. Water in a dry summer. Support taller varieties in windy positions. Cut down dead stems in late autumn, protect crowns with compost. Divide every 4–5 years.
Propagation:	Divide in early spring.
Recommended:	Many including 'Queen Charlotte', 'Bressingham Glow'.
Useful tip:	Divided plants take at least a season to start flowering.
Related plants:	A. hupehensis hybrids: 'Hadspen Abundance', 'Prince Heinrich'.

10

Anthemis tinctoria Dyer's Chamomile, Golden Marguerite

Flowering time: Early summer to early autumn.

Height: 60–90cm (2–3ft).

Spread: 38–45cm (15–18in).

Soil: Light, dry, well-drained.

Positioning: Full sun, sheltered from wind; 45cm (18in) apart in bold groups in mid-border or on a bank.

Care: Plant in autumn or spring in well-dug soil and dress with general fertilizer. Feed with general fertilizer in spring and just before flowering. Support flower stems in exposed sites and cut down exhausted ones to encourage new growth at the base.

Propagation: Divide in spring; grow cuttings under glass in summer.

Recommended: Basic species and white 'Alba', 'E. C. Buxton' (soft lemon), 'Grallach Gold'.

Useful tip: Plants decline in vigour after 2–3 years, so take cuttings regularly.

Related plants: A. marschalliana, compact gold form for rock gardens; similar white A. carpatica.

ANTHEMIS TINCTORIA

This showy clump-forming species has been grown for centuries as a staple dye plant, although several hybrids are now available that make fine cut flowers as well as vigorous, if short-lived, garden plants. They deserve to be massed in generous groups, ideally near grey-leafed plants or beside old-fashioned roses.

AQUILEGIA VULGARIS 'NORA BARLOW'

One of the easiest of all perennials, Aquilegia quickly establishes itself in most gardens where it will seed freely; the plain pink or blue seedlings tend to outnumber coloured hybrids. All kinds have extremely decorative foliage, even after the flowers have finished in high summer, and strong roots that search deeply for water.

Flowering time: Late spring to mid-summer.

Height: 15cm–1.2m (6in–4ft).

Spread: 30–60cm (1–2ft).

Soil: Any very well-drained soil.

Positioning: Sun or shade (best in light dappled shade); 30–45cm (12–18in) apart in groups in borders or shaded corners; naturalized in wild gardens.

Care: Plant in autumn or spring in lightly dug soil with added general fertilizer. Mulch with compost in late spring. Water freely in dry weather. Deadhead, and liquid feed after flowering. Cut down growth in autumn.

Propagation: Divide in spring or autumn.

Recommended: Basic species and many hybrids like 'Alpine Blue', Crimson Star', variegated Vervaeneana Group.

Useful tip: Watch out for aphids at flowering time and spray with insecticide.

Related plants: Many lovely species including *A. chrysantha* 'Yellow Queen', dwarf *A. flabellata* 'Mini-star'.

Flowering time: Mid-summer to early autumn.

Height: 75–90cm (30–36in).

Spread: 60–75cm (24–30in).

Soil: Dryish, well-drained.

Positioning: Full sun, sheltered from strong winds; singly or 60cm (2ft) apart in groups, in borders and containers.

Care: Plant in spring in well-dug soil with added grit for efficient drainage; dress with bonemeal. Support with twiggy sticks in exposed places. In mid-spring cut down top growth to about 30cm (12in) and feed with high-potash fertilizer.

Propagation: Divide in spring; grow cuttings under glass in summer.

Recommended: Basic species and selections var. *incompta,* var. *latiloba,* and varieties 'Silver Queen', 'Valerie Finnis'.

Useful tip: Running roots may infiltrate other plants; trim to size with a spade if necessary.

Related plants: *A. absinthium* 'Lambrook Silver'; *A.* 'Powis Castle'.

Most Artemisias love sunny dry sites where the silver or grey leaves, which are often aromatic, assume the clearest colours and plants are safe from winter wetness around their roots. They make fine specimens whether grown as highlights or to accompany bright perennial flowers. As a bonus, the foliage and seedheads may be cut for dried bouquets.

Flowering time:	Early to late summer.
Height:	20cm–1.2m (8in–4ft) according to variety.
Spread:	20–90cm (8in–3ft).
Soil:	Moist, leafy (not clay or chalk).
Positioning:	Light shade; singly or 15–60cm (6in–2ft) apart, in front or mid-border and in bog gardens.
Care:	Plant in autumn or spring, in well-dug soil with plenty of compost or decayed manure. Water thoroughly in dry weather. Cut down all growth in autumn (or spring), and mulch with compost or manure. Divide every 3–4 years.
Propagation:	Divide in mid-autumn or spring; sow under glass in spring.
Recommended:	A. × arendsii hybrids, especially 'Amethyst', 'Bridal Veil', 'Cattleya' 'Fanal', 'Feuer', 'Weisse Gloria'.
Useful tip:	A. chinensis var. pumila, 'Purple Lance' and 'Superba' are good in drier soils.
Related plants:	A. simplicifolia hybrids. A. thunbergii hybrids, tall with slender arching flowers.

ASTILBE × ARENDSII 'SPARTAN'

Astilbes flourish in marshy soil where few other border perennials can survive, and are the perfect choice for bog gardens and pond-side planting. There are many enticing kinds, from sturdy rock garden miniatures to large vigorous types with tall elegant plumes that sometimes arch down.

Flowering time: Early to late summer.

Height: 60–90cm (2–3ft).

Spread: 45–60cm (18–24in).

Soil: Moist, fertile, alkaline (not heavy clay).

Positioning: Light or semi-shade; 30cm (12in) apart in a moist border or bog garden.

Care: Plant in autumn or spring in well-dug soil with plenty of compost or decayed manure, and lime in acid soils. Feed with general fertilizer in spring, and mulch dry soils with compost. Water freely in dry weather. Support plants in exposed sites. Cut down growth in autumn.

Propagation: Divide in late autumn or early spring; sow in a frame in mid-spring.

Recommended: Basic species and *rosea, rubra.* 'Sunningdale Variegated' (syn. 'Variegata'), for dappled sunlight.

Useful tip: Slugs and snails like the young foliage.

Related plants: *A maxima,* tall with large pink blooms; *A. carniolica* var. *rubra.*

ASTRANTIA MAJOR 'SUNNINGDALE VARIEGATED'

Astrantia is one of the oldest cottage garden flowers, with attractive foliage and subtly coloured blooms that last well in water and may be dried for winter decoration. With their modest and yet fascinating appearance, plants should be grown well away from more flamboyant neighbours.

15

BERGENIA CORDIFOLIA 'ABENDGLOCKEN'

This large leathery species is one of the parents of many modern hybrids, all of which are popular for their ease of cultivation and tolerance of almost any situation. The magnificent flower heads are a welcome sight in spring and, together with the autumn leaves that add rich colours to indoor arrangements, are a favourite for cutting.

Flowering time:	Late winter to late spring, sometimes again in early autumn
Height:	30–45cm (12–18in).
Spread:	45–60cm (18–24in).
Soil:	Any fertile, well-drained soil.
Positioning:	Full sun or semi-shade 30cm (12in) apart at the front of borders, b water, as ground cover.
Care:	Plant in autumn or spring in well-dug soil with added bonemea Water on dry soils; mulch with compost before flowering. Deadhead; clear dea leaves. Trim sprawling stems back at any time; divide every 4–6 years.
Propagation:	Divide after flowering or in autumn and replant rooted portions
Recommended:	Basic species and darker forms 'Purpurea and 'Redstart'; hybrids like 'Silberlicht' (syn. 'Silver Light'), 'Bressingham White'.
Useful tip:	Grow with blue flowe like *Brunnera*.
Related plants:	*B. crassifolia* and 'Autumn Red'; dark *B. purpurascens*; rose-pink *B. × schmidtii*.

Flowering time: Early to late summer.

Height: 45cm–1.2m (18in–4ft), according to variety.

Spread: 30–60cm (12–24in).

Soil: Any well-drained soil.

Positioning: Full sun or partial shade; as solo highlights or 23–45cm (9–18in) apart in groups in mid-border.

Care: Plant in autumn or spring in lightly dug soil with added lime if acid, grit on heavy ground. Feed in spring with general fertilizer. Water in dry weather on very light soils. Support tall varieties. Deadhead to prolong display.

Propagation: Divide in autumn or spring; grow cuttings or sow in a frame in spring.

Recommended: C. lactiflora 'Loddon Anna', 'Prichard's Variety', 'White Pouffe'; C. latifolia 'Gloaming', 'White Ladies'; C. persicifolia 'Fleur de Neige', 'Pride of Exmouth'.

Useful tip: Protect against slugs in moist shaded positions.

Related plants: C. glomerata, especially 'Superba'.

CAMPANULA LACTIFLORA

This is a huge race of perennials, with star- or bell-shaped flowers in shades of blue, pink or white. Most borders depend on one or more species for summer colour, especially the taller kinds with slender graceful stems and a habit of sowing themselves in any suitable niche.

CENTAUREA MONTANA ALBA

Cornflowers are good survivors, adapted to dry and impoverished sites where they flower more prolifically than under more lavish growing conditions. The bright thistle-like blooms are popular for cutting, and make a bold display on their own or as part of a mixed border scheme.

Flowering time: Late spring to mid-summer.

Height: 45–90cm (18in–3ft).

Spread: 90cm (3ft).

Soil: Light, dry, alkaline.

Positioning: Full sun or very light shade; 45cm (18in) apart in groups in mid-border.

Care: Plant in autumn or spring in lightly forked soil with added bonemeal, and lime if acid. Feed in spring with general fertilizer; after flowering mulch with compost or leaf mould. Support stems of taller varieties. Deadhead. Cut growth to ground in autumn. Divide every 3 years.

Propagation: Divide in autumn or spring; sow outdoors in spring.

Recommended: *C. dealbata*, basic pink species and crimson 'Steenbergii'; pink *C. hypoleuca* 'John Coutts'; *C. montana*, basic blue species, *alba*.

Useful tip: Plants that are dead-headed and fed after flowering may bloom again in autumn.

Related plants: *C. macrocephala*, yellow, tall stems.

Centranthus ruber Red Valerian

lowering time: Early to mid-summer, intermittently to early autumn.

Height: 45–90cm (18in–3ft).

Spread: 45–90cm (18in–3ft).

Soil: Any dryish soil.

Positioning: Full sun or very light shade; singly or 38cm (15in) apart in groups, in mid-border, beside paths and on walls.

Care: Plant in autumn or spring in lightly forked soil with added bonemeal. Feed in spring with general fertilizer. Water now and then in prolonged hot weather. Trim by half after main flowering for autumn display; cut down all growth in late autumn or early spring.

Propagation: Sow in a frame in late summer or spring; grow cuttings under glass in spring.

Recommended: Basic species and red *atrococcineus*, white *albus*, rose *coccineus* (often all available in a seed mixture).

Useful tip: Remove seedlings to control spread or transplant while small.

Related plants: *Valeriana officinalis*, pink or white.

CENTRANTHUS RUBER

Often found growing out from dry walls and banks, this old cottage garden flower seems to thrive on very little, its tough penetrating roots extracting nourishment from the most inhospitable sites. Flowering is prolific, followed by fluffy seeds that colonize any available crack or crevice. (syn. *Kentranthus*.)

CLEMATIS × ERIOSTEMON

Shrubby forms of clematis are quite unlike their climbing cousins except in the length and intensity of their flowering season. Blooms are often fragrant and richly coloured, and make a stunning display among grey-leafed shrubs, while the plants are among some of the easiest to grow and prune.

Flowering time: Early summer to early autumn, according to variety.

Height: 60cm–1.5m (2–5ft).

Spread: 60cm–1.2m (2–4ft).

Soil: Moist, well-drained.

Positioning: Full sun or light shade; as specimen plants with some support in a container, border.

Care: Plant in spring in deeply dug soil with plenty of compost, lime in acid soils; mix grit in heavy ground to aid drainage. Liquid feed regularly. Water in dry weather. Mulch with decayed manure in autumn. Support stems on twigs, trellis or shrubs. Shorten growth by half or cut almost to ground level in autumn or spring.

Propagation: Divide in autumn or spring; grow cuttings in a frame in spring.

Recommended: C. heracleifolia 'Côte d'Azur', 'Wyevale'; C. integrifolia 'Rosea'; C. recta, basic species, 'Purpurea'.

Useful tip: Top up mulches to keep roots cool and moist.

Related plants: C. × eriostemon and C. × durandii, taller.

owering time: Mid- to late spring.

Height: 15–23cm (6–9in).

Spread: Up to 45cm (18in).

Soil: Deep, moist, leafy.

Positioning: Light or semi-shade; 20cm (8in) apart in large groups at border edges, as ground cover under shrubs.

Care: Plant in autumn in well-dug soil with plenty of compost or decayed manure: spread roots horizontally 5cm (2in) deep. Water now and then in dry weather. Mulch in autumn with compost or leaf mould. Hand-weed only (plants resent cultivation). Vigorous clumps may be divided every 4–5 years.

Propagation: Divide in mid-autumn; sow in a frame in late summer.

ecommended: Basic species and pink var. *rosea*, large-flowered 'Fortin's Giant', variegated 'Albostriata' and var. *variegata*.

Useful tip: Roots dislike being disturbed so divide them using a spade to chop out large sods; replant the sods intact.

Related plants: None.

CONVALLARIA MAJALIS

Lily-of-the-valley is one of the most popular old-fashioned perennials, energetic in moist shade and always welcome in spring when each pair of fresh green leaves opens to reveal an arching stem of white bells. The fragrance of the flowers is renowned, and a small bouquet will scent a room for many days.

Corydalis lutea Yellow Fumitory

CORYDALIS LUTEA

The dainty arching foliage of *Corydalis lutea* is as pretty as any fern, while numerous stalks, all twisting to face the same way, bear bright yellow spurred flowers – almost all season in light shade. Some gardeners consider this tenacious perennial to be a weed, but that is to underestimate its charm and value. (syn. *Pseudofumaria lutea*.)

Flowering time:	Mid-spring to early autumn.
Height:	15–30cm (6–12in).
Spread:	30cm (12in).
Soil:	Any slightly fertile, well drained soil.
Positioning:	Full sun or shade (light shade to prolong flowering); in crevices in walls, paving cracks, 23cm (9in) apart as edging, ground cover.
Care:	In spring plant or sow in situ in lightly forked soil with added bonemeal. Feed in spring with general fertilizer. Plants are quite undemanding, but cut back promptly after flowering to prevent lavish self-seeding. Clear all top growth in late autumn.
Propagation:	Sow under glass or in situ in spring; divide clumps in spring.
Recommended:	Basic species and white 'Alba' (syn. *Pseudofumaria alba*).
Useful tip:	Gather stems at any time for small vases.
Related plants:	C. cashmeriana (bright blue), rockeries; C. flexuosa 'China Blue'; C. solida; C. wilsonii.

Crambe cordifolia Giant Sea Kale

Flowering time: Early to late summer.
Height: Up to 1.8m (6ft).
Spread: 1.2m (4ft).
Soil: Deep, moist (but not waterlogged).
Positioning: Full sun; as a specimen plant against a dark wall or at the back of a border.
Care: Plant in autumn or spring in deeply dug soil with plenty of compost. Feed with general fertilizer in spring and mulch with compost. Water in dry weather; feed with high-potash fertilizer after flowering. Cut down to ground level in autumn.
Propagation: Divide in autumn or spring; sow in a frame in spring.
Recommended: Basic species only.
Useful tip: As its common name implies, this is an excellent plant for seaside gardens.
Related plants: C. koktebelica, huge flower heads; C. maritima (Sea Kale), compact with edible stems and more elegant flowers; G. tatarica, tall with edible roots.

CRAMBE CORDIFOLIA

These low-growing plants with their broad heart-shaped leaves up to 90cm (3ft) long are impressive even when they are not in flower. In summer a tall tangled mass of flower stems erupts in a huge cloud of tiny white honey-scented blooms. Single plants make imposing features, while a small group is magnificent but space-consuming.

Flowering time: Mid-summer to early autumn.

Height: 60cm–1.2m (2–4ft).

Spread: 23–30cm (9–12in).

Soil: Light, dry, rich.

Positioning: Full sun, in a warm sheltered site; 15cm (6in) apart in large groups in open borders, at the foot of a wall.

Care: Plant corms in spring, 8cm (3in) deep in well dug soil with added bonemeal; work grit into heavy ground. Water well in early summer, feed once or twice with high-potash fertilizer. Mulch with leaf mould or bracken in autumn. Cut back foliage in spring.

Propagation: Divide in early spring or autumn; sow species seeds in a frame in spring.

Recommended: C. x crocosmiiflora hybrids like 'Ember Glow', 'Citronella'.

Useful tip: In cold gardens lift corms in late autumn and store in a frost-proof place.

Related plants: C. masoniorum, 'Dixter Flame', 'Firebird'; C. paniculata (Giant Montbretia).

CROCOSMIA × CROCOSMIIFLORA HYBRID

Many brightly coloured and large-flowered hybrids of montbretia, an old-fashioned plant of cottage gardens, are now available. They provide a welcome splash of colour in autumn, especially when planted *en masse*, but are not fully hardy in very cold gardens.

Delphinium hybrids <small>Delphinium</small>

Flowering time: Early and mid-summer, often again in early or mid-autumn.

Height: Up to 1.8m (6ft).

Spread: 75cm (30in).

Soil: Moist, but never waterlogged.

Positioning: Full sun, sheltered from wind; 60–75cm (2–2½ft) apart at the back of borders.

Care: Plant in spring in deeply dug soil with plenty of compost, and grit for drainage on heavy soils. Feed in spring with general fertilizer. Water well in dry weather. Support with strong canes at an early stage. Trim back stems when summer flowers finish and feed again. Cut to ground in late autumn. Divide every few years.

Propagation: Divide in spring; grow cuttings under glass in mid-spring.

Recommended: Pacific Giants; D. × belladonna 'Cliveden Beauty'.

Useful tip: Spray with systemic fungicide if heat and dry air cause mildew.

Related plants: D. grandiflorum 'Blue Butterfly', often raised as an annual.

DELPHINIUM 'BLUE DAWN'

Stately blue delphiniums are a classic feature of summer borders: their tall spires, densely packed with large blooms, tower above neighbouring plants. An already wide range is extended by dwarf types, an increasing number of pink and red varieties, and slender airy *elatum* and *belladonna* strains. (syn. *D.* × *cultorum*.)

DICENTRA SPECTABILIS

This cottage garden perennial can reach an impressive size if it is planted in a bright moist position. Grow it in the cool shade of shrubs and trees, where its pretty foliage and long flower stems decked with perfectly shaped lockets will be summer highlights.

Flowering time: Late spring to mid-summer.

Height: 45–60cm (18–24in).

Spread: 45cm (18in).

Soil: Moist, light.

Positioning: Dappled sunlight or light shade, sheltered from winds; singly or 30cm apart in groups, in borders, as ground cover in shrubberies.

Care: Plant in autumn or spring in deeply dug soil with added compost or leaf mould, and grit to improve drainage. Feed with general fertilizer in spring and after flowering. Water in dry weather. Protect from slugs. Mulch in autumn or late spring with compost or leaf mould.

Propagation: Divide in autumn or spring; sow under glass in spring.

Recommended: Basic species and white 'Alba'; also hybrids 'Adrian Bloom', 'Luxuriant'.

Useful tip: The roots are very brittle: do not disturb plants unnecessarily.

Related plants: *D. formosa*, especially 'Stuart Boothman'; *D. eximia* 'Snowdrift'.

Dictamnus albus Dittany, Burning Bush

Flowering time: Early to late summer.

Height: 60–75cm (24–30in).

Spread: 30–45cm (12–18in).

Soil: Dry, well-drained (not heavy clay).

Positioning: Full sun or very light shade, sheltered from winds; singly or 30cm (12in) apart, at the front of borders, in a herb garden.

Care: Plant in autumn or spring in well-dug soil with added compost and bonemeal. Feed with high-potash fertilizer in spring. Water in dry weather. Deadhead after flowering. Cut to ground level in mid-autumn, and mulch with compost or leaves. Divide every 4–5 years.

Propagation: Divide in autumn or spring; sow outdoors in late summer.

Recommended: Basic species and lilac-pink var. *purpureus*.

Useful tip: Plants may take a season to settle down, especially when they are planted in spring.

Related plants: Other species are now reclassified as forms of *D. albus*.

DICTAMNUS ALBUS

This is a favourite ornamental herb and border plant that has been cultivated since Roman times. Its aromatic leaves smell of lemons or balsam, depending on how much they are bruised, and the fragrant spidery flowers exude oils that can be ignited with a match on warm dry days.

Dierama pulcherrimum Wand Flower, Angels' Fishing Rods

DIERAMA PULCHERRIMUM

The stems of these fine bulbs are tall and slender, and their tips arch gracefully to allow the long tassels of bell-like flowers to sway in the breeze. When reflected in nearby water, they produce a stunning, almost hypnotic, ballet of gentle movements. The dwarf forms are valuable for more exposed positions.

Flowering time: Late summer to mid-autumn.

Height: 75cm–1.5m (2½–5ft)

Spread: 30cm (12in).

Soil: Deep, rich, dry, well-drained.

Positioning: Full sun, sheltered from wind; 10–15cm (4–6in) apart in group in mid-border, by warm walls, ponds.

Care: Plant bulbs in late autumn, 8cm (3in) deep in deeply dug soil with added compost, and grit if drainage is poor. Feed with general fertilizer in spring, mid-summer. In autumn cut to the ground. Mulch with composted bark or leaves over winter. Divide every 4–5 years.

Propagation: Divide in late autumn; sow under glass in spring.

Recommended: Basic species; also Slieve Donard hybrids.

Useful tip: Seedlings may be easier to establish than divisions.

Related plants: Shorter *D. pendulum*, basic species and 'Puck'; dwarf *D. dracomontanum* (syn. *D. pumilum*).

28

wering time:	Early to late summer.
Height:	90cm–1.8m (3–6ft).
Spread:	30–45cm (12–18in).
Soil:	Ideally moist; dry soil tolerated.
Positioning:	Best in semi-shade (tolerates full sun), sheltered from strong winds; 30cm (12in) apart in groups in borders and wild or herb gardens.
Care:	Plant in autumn or early spring in deeply dug soil with plenty of compost or leaf mould. Feed with general fertilizer in spring and after flowering; mulch in spring with compost or leaf mould. Water in dry weather. Deadhead or let self-sow; cut to the leaf rosette in autumn.
Propagation:	Sow in situ or in a frame in spring.
commended:	D. purpurea, white form albiflora, Excelsior Hybrids, 'The Shirley'; D. grandiflora; D. × mertonensis.
Useful tip:	Cut stems for vases when one-third of the blooms are open.
elated plants:	D. ferruginea and D. lanata, for sunny dry positions.

DIGITALIS PURPUREA 'SUTTON'S APRICOT'

Foxgloves are easy-going plants that adapt happily to most positions. There are many desirable kinds, some of which survive for many years – the yellow species is an example. The common purple foxglove is usually biennial but will revive for a few seasons if it is prevented from seeding.

DORONICUM × EXCELSUM 'HARPUR CREWE'

The yellow or gold blooms of Doronicum, up to 8cm (3in) across in some forms, appear before other perennials have fully revived and illuminate the spring garden with bold splashes of radiant colour. They are classic cottage garden flowers and surprisingly under-valued, perhaps because they are so undemanding.

Flowering time: Mid-spring to early summer.

Height: 50–90cm (20in–3ft).

Spread: 60cm (2ft).

Soil: Any fertile soil.

Positioning: Full sun or semi-shade, singly or 38–45cm (15–18in) apart in small groups, at the front of borders, foot of walls.

Care: Plant in autumn or spring in well-dug soil with added compost, leaf mould. Feed with general fertilizer in spring and after flowering. Water in dry weather. Support taller varieties. Deadhead regularly. Cut down all growth late autumn. Divide every 3 years.

Propagation: Divide in spring or autumn; sow in a frame in spring.

Recommended: *D. orientale* (syn. *D. caucasicum*) and 'Finesse'; *D. × excelsum* 'Harpur Crewe', 'Miss Mason'.

Useful tip: Prompt deadheading can stimulate more flowers in autumn.

Related plants: Dwarf *D. orientale* 'Goldzwerg', for rock gardens.

Flowering time: Early summer to early autumn.

Height: 90cm–1.2m (3–4ft).

Spread: 45–60cm (18–24in).

Soil: Rich, moist, leafy, with good drainage.

Positioning: Full sun or light shade (may adapt to semi-shade); 45cm (18in) apart, in the middle or back of borders.

Care: Plant in autumn or spring in deeply dug soil with plenty of compost or leaf mould. Feed with general fertilizer in spring and mid-summer; on dry soils mulch in late spring with compost or leaf mould. Water in dry weather. Support in windy sites. Deadhead regularly, cutting exhausted stems to their base. Divide every 3–4 years.

Propagation: Divide in autumn or spring; sow in a frame in spring.

Recommended: Basic species and Bressingham Hybrids, 'White Lustre'.

Useful tip: Grow behind pink *Sidalcea* for impact.

Related plants: *E. angustifolia*, medicinal, for herb gardens.

ECHINACEA PURPUREA

These stately prairie plants from North America are remarkably vigorous and bloom over a long season. Their brightly coloured daisies, up to 10cm (4in) across, are distinguished by a prominent raised disc or cone in the centre, from which the rose, purple or white petals seem to droop languidly. (syn. *Rudbeckia purpurea*.)

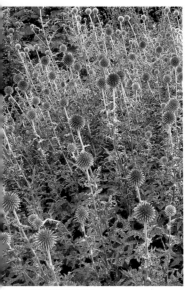

ECHINOPS BANNATICUS

Flowering time: Early to late summer.
Height: 90cm–1.5m (3–5ft).
Spread: 60cm (2ft) or more.
Soil: Any well-drained soil.
Positioning: Full sun; singly or 45cm (18in) apart in small groups, in mid-border, at the foot of sunny hedges.
Care: Plant in autumn or spring in deeply dug soil with added compost; work in plenty of grit if drainage is poor. Support while young, before stems begin to lean. Deadhead regularly; cut down a growth in late autumn; trim round clumps with a spade to limit spread.
Propagation: Divide in autumn or spring; sow in a frame in late spring.
Recommended: *E. ritro* and darker 'Veitch's Blue'.
Useful tip: Cut when the first flowers open, and dry them for indoor decoration in winter.
Related plants: *E. bannaticus*, and 'Blue Globe', 'Taplow Blue', taller with large flower heads.

Planted *en masse*, these robust summer flowers produce thickets of richly coloured blooms that attract bees in huge numbers. They prefer dryish soils and low fertility, and are ideal for low-maintenance gardens. Some varieties are very prickly (the botanical name comes from the Greek word for 'hedgehog'), so wear gloves when handling them.

pimedium grandiflorum Bishop's Hat, Bishop's Mitre

owering time: Mid-spring to early summer.

Height: 30–38cm (12–15in).

Spread: 45–60cm (18–24in).

Soil: Any well-drained soil.

Positioning: Partial or full shade; 30cm (12in) apart as dense ground cover under shrubs and trees, at the front of shady borders, as edging.

Care: Plant in autumn or spring in well-dug soil with added compost or leaf mould; add plenty of grit to heavy soils. Water regularly in the first year. Leave old foliage in place over winter, cut down in early spring and feed with general fertilizer or mulch with compost. Divide every 3–4 years.

Propagation: Divide in autumn or spring.

ecommended: Basic species, dwarf 'Nanum', 'White Queen'.

Useful tip: Cut autumn foliage for indoor arrangements.

Related plants: *E. × youngianum* 'Niveum'; *E. × rubrum*; *E. × versicolor* 'Sulphureum'; *E. × perralchium* and 'Frohnleiten'.

EPIMEDIUM GRANDIFLORUM 'VIOLET SEEDLING'

These plants are slow-growing at first, but spread into dense semi-evergreen ground cover with small attractive flowers early in the year. Their real glory is the progressive change in their leaf colour, from bronze-yellow with pink veins in spring to rich chestnut red in autumn.

ERIGERON KARVINSKIANUS

This little Mexican daisy will seed itself in the most unlikely places once it has been introduced in the garden. Grow a few plants as edging, and watch them colonize steps, dry walls, gravel paths and other inhospitable niches. It is always charming and is easily removed should it spread too far. (syn. *E. mucronatus*.)

Flowering time:	Early summer to mid-autumn.
Height:	Up to 23cm (9in).
Spread:	30cm (12in).
Soil:	Any well-drained soil.
Positioning:	Full sun (best for flowers) or semi-shade 30cm (12in) apart in small groups as edging to borders and paths, between paving stones and on walls.
Care:	Plant in spring in lightly dug soil with added bonemeal; work grit into heavy soil. Water in dry weather until established. Deadhead. Trim back long stems in late autumn; protect with a gravel mulch in cold gardens.
Propagation:	Divide in spring; sow under glass or in situ in spring.
Recommended:	Basic species only.
Useful tip:	In cold wet soil, split plants in autumn and keep divisions in a frame over winter.
Related plants:	*E. speciosus* hybrids like 'Dignity', 'Darkest of All', 'Foersters Liebling', 'Pink Jewel', 'Snow White', 'Schwarzes Meer' (syn. 'Black Sea').

Euphorbia myrsinites Myrtle Spurge

Flowering time: Early spring to mid-summer.

Height: 15–20cm (6–8in).

Spread: Up to 60cm (24in).

Soil: Any dry soil with very good drainage.

Positioning: Full sun; 38–45cm (15–18in) apart as edging to borders, in rock gardens, low walls.

Care: Plant in spring or early summer in well-dug soil with added bonemeal. Feed in mid-spring with general fertilizer. Deadhead after flowering. Divide every 3–4 years or when stems become very woody.

Propagation: Divide in mid-spring; grow cuttings in a frame in spring.

Recommended: Basic species only.

Useful tip: After a cold wet winter, cut back any damaged stems to healthy tissue and feed well.

Related plants: Shade-tolerant: *E. amygdaloides*; *E. griffithii* 'Dixter', 'Fireglow' (red); tall *E. sikkimensis*. Bog gardens: *E. palustris* (Swamp Spurge). Full sun: *E. polychroma*; prostrate *E. capitulata*.

EUPHORBIA MYRSINITES

The tiny flowers of this perennial are surrounded by coloured bracts, or modified leaves, which last for many weeks and may be cut for indoor decoration. It is just one member of a huge family, almost all of which are robust, evergreen and slightly succulent, with a milky sap that can be irritating to the skin.

GAILLARDIA 'GOBLIN'

On a hot sunny site this popular Mexican plant produces a showy display for several years, and there are many hybrids with vivid flowers up to 10cm (4in) across to brighten the border all season. Shade and damp may be lethal though, and cuttings should be overwintered in a frame as an insurance against loss.

Flowering time:	Early summer to mid-autumn.
Height:	Up to 90cm (3ft).
Spread:	45cm (18in).
Soil:	Light, dry, well-drained.
Positioning:	Full sun, sheltered from spring frosts; 45cm (18in) apart, in bold groups near the front of borders, beside walls.
Care:	Plant in spring in well-dug soil with a little added compost and plenty of grit to aid drainage. Feed in spring with general fertilizer. Support tall varieties with twiggy sticks. Deadhead regularly. Cut down stems in late autumn.
Propagation:	Grow cuttings in a frame in late summer; divide in early spring; sow under glass or in a frame in spring.
Recommended:	Many fine varieties, including 'Burgundy', 'Dazzler', 'Goblin' (syn. 'Kobold'), 'Mandarin', 'Wirral Flame'.
Useful tip:	Divide every 3 years to keep plants vigorous.
Related plants:	G. × grandiflora 'Aurea Plena', strong double yellow.

Flowering time: Early to late summer.

Height: 60–90cm (2–3ft).

Spread: Up to 60cm (2ft).

Soil: Leafy, moist (not waterlogged).

Positioning: Light or semi-shade; 38–45cm (15–18in) apart beside shrubs and trees, near water, in cool borders.

Care: Plant in spring in deeply dug soil with plenty of compost or leaf mould. Feed with general fertilizer in spring and mid-summer. Water regularly in a dry season. Support with twiggy sticks on exposed sites. Cut down growth in mid-autumn.

Propagation: Divide in spring; sow in a frame in mid-autumn.

Recommended: Basic species and white *alba*, 'Nymans', 'Phyllis', 'Rosea' (pink).

Useful tip: Avoid positioning plants where overhead branches drip on them as they may rot.

Related plants: Autumn-flowering *G. sino-ornata*; *G. lutea*, sunny dry sites, slow-growing.

GENTIANA ASCLEPIADEA

Some gentians are difficult to grow, but this tall vigorous species is undemanding if grown in the right position. Given the moisture and shade it loves it can be left virtually untended, for it resents disturbance and takes time to settle after planting or division.

GERANIUM PRATENSE

You could collect dozens of different geraniums and still not exhaust the huge range of desirable varieties. These are not the tender pelargoniums of summer bedding schemes, but hardy herbaceous plants with mounds of shapely foliage and large bright single blooms. Grown formally or naturalized as ground cover, they are some of the easiest border plants.

Flowering time: Late spring to late summer.
Height: Up to 75cm (30in).
Spread: 45cm (18in).
Soil: Any free-draining soil.
Positioning: Full sun or semi-shade; 38–45cm (15–18in) apart in groups as ground cover, near the front of borders and naturalized in wild gardens.
Care: Plant in autumn or spring in deeply dug soil with a little compost. Feed with general fertilizer in spring and after flowering. Protect while young from slugs. Water regularly until established. Support tall varieties with peasticks. Cut to ground level in autumn.
Propagation: Divide in spring.
Recommended: G. endressii; G. macrorrhizum 'Album', 'Ingwersen's Variety'; G. pratense; G. 'Johnson's Blue'; G. psilostemon 'Bressingham Flair'.
Useful tip: Shear off foliage after flowering for a second flush of bloom.
Related plants: Erodium (Storksbill), similar, many forms.

Geum chiloense (Garden) Avens

lowering time: Late spring to mid-summer.

Height: 45–60cm (18–24in).

Spread: 45cm (18in).

Soil: Moist, fertile.

Positioning: Full sun or very light shade; 38–45cm (15–18in) apart in groups of 3 near the front of borders, massed as ground cover.

Care: Plant in autumn or spring in deeply dug soil with plenty of compost or decayed manure. Feed in spring with general fertilizer. Water well when dry. Support flowering stems with twiggy sticks. Deadhead regularly. Cut to ground level at the end of the season. Divide every 4–5 years.

Propagation: Divide in autumn or spring; sow in a frame in spring.

Recommended: 'Georgenberg', 'Lady Stratheden', 'Mrs. J. Bradshaw'; also G. 'Borisii'.

Useful tip: Cut back and feed after main flowering for a second flush.

Related plants: G. rivale, bog gardens.

GEUM CHILOENSE 'DOLLY NORTH'

The impact of this short-lived perennial is memorable, especially when plants are grouped together in lavish patches. The relatively small flowers are bowl- or bell-shaped, many of them semi-double, and radiate colour in the early summer border.

Gypsophila paniculata Baby's Breath

GYPSOPHILA PANICULATA

Gypsophila is the most effective companion for brightly coloured flowers, whether in the garden or indoors as part of an arrangement. Although an old-fashioned plant, it never fails to impress: when grown well, a mature specimen makes a billowing cloud of white or pale pink for many weeks.

Flowering time: Early to late summer.
Height: Up to 1.2m (4ft).
Spread: 1.2m (4ft).
Soil: Dry, fertile (not acid).
Positioning: Full sun; singly or 90cm (3ft) apart as mid-border highlights; shorter forms as edging.
Care: Plant in autumn or spring in deeply dug soil with added bonemeal, and lime if acid. Feed with general fertilizer in spring and at the start and end of flowering. Support tall forms with peasticks. Cut to ground level in autumn.
Propagation: Grow cuttings under glass in late spring; sow in a frame in spring.
Recommended: Basic species and 'Bristol Fairy', 'Compacta Plena', 'Snowflake'; also G. 'Rosenshleier' (syn. 'Veil of Roses').
Useful tip: Plants resent being disturbed: do not move or try to divide established specimens.
Related plants: Prostrate or trailing G. repens, and 'Dorothy Teacher', 'Dubia', 'Rosea'.

Flowering time: Early summer to mid-autumn.

Height: Up to 90cm–1.2m (3–4ft).

Spread: 60–75cm (2–2½ft).

Soil: Moist, rich, with good drainage.

Positioning: Full sun or very light shade; 60cm (2ft) apart in the middle and back of borders.

Care: Plant in autumn or spring in deeply dug soil with plenty of compost. Feed in spring with general fertilizer, and mulch with compost. Water in dry weather. Support tall varieties. Deadhead occasionally. Cut to ground level in late autumn.

Propagation: Divide in autumn or spring.

Recommended: 'Bruno', 'Butterpat', 'Crimson Beauty', 'Moerheim Beauty', 'Pumilum Magnificum', 'Waldtraut'.

Useful tip: The quality of the plants deteriorates; replace every few years.

Related plants: H. bigelovii, dark yellow; H. hoopesii, golden-yellow.

HELENIUM 'MOERHEIM BEAUTY'

This is just one of many handsome varieties that have surpassed their parent species H. autumnale in colour and vigour. There are tall and dwarf, early or late-flowering kinds, all long-lived and prolific, and indispensable for an impressive display in the late summer garden. Colours can be very intense, so choose carefully to avoid strident clashes.

HELLEBORUS ORIENTALIS

These undemanding and extraordinarily long-lived perennials are a priority for early colour in the garden. The semi-evergreen plants bear large blooms, often 8cm (3in) across, in a range of colours with subtle differences that are especially noticeable in self-sown seedlings.

Flowering time: Late winter to mid-spring.

Height: 45–60cm (18–24in).

Spread: 60cm (24in).

Soil: Deep, fertile (not acid) soil.

Positioning: Full sun or semi-shade sheltered from winter winds; singly or 45cm (18in) apart in groups under shrubs, trees and at the front of borders, in shady corners.

Care: Plant in autumn or spring in deeply dug soil with plenty of compost, and lime if acid. Feed with bonemeal after flowering, mulch with compost. Water regularly in dry weather. Protect against slugs. Tidy dead foliage at the end of winter.

Propagation: Divide in autumn or spring; sow in a frame in autumn.

Recommended: 'Little Black' and ssp. *guttatus*; Ballard's Group, Hadspen Hybrids.

Useful tip: Grow with snowdrops for a spring display.

Related plants: *H. niger* and its varieties; forms of *H. foetidus*.

wering time: Early summer to early autumn.

Height: 45cm–1.2m (18in–4ft).

Spread: 30–45cm (12–18in).

Soil: Moist, fertile.

Positioning: Full sun or very light shade; 38–45cm (15–18in) apart in groups in the middle or back of borders, as edging to paths.

Care: Plant in autumn or spring in deeply dug soil with plenty of compost. Water thoroughly in dry weather. Feed in spring and mid-summer with general fertilizer; mulch with decayed manure in late autumn.

Propagation: Divide in autumn or spring.

ommended: 'Cartwheels', 'Golden Chimes', 'Black Magic', 'Bonanza', 'Whichford', 'Pink Damask', 'Stafford'.

Useful tip: Plants are best left undisturbed until flowering begins to decline.

lated plants: Fragrant *H. citrina* (Lily-of-the-Valley Day Lily, Lemon Day Lily); *H. lilioasphodelus*; *H. minor*.

HEMEROCALLIS 'YESTERDAY'S MEMORIES'

Literally hundreds of fine hybrids offer a bewildering choice of this resilient and trouble-free favourite. Tall and dwarf forms are available, with blooms up to 20cm (8in) across; each lasts for just a day but is followed by a generous succession of further blooms.

Heuchera hybrids Coral Bells, Coral Flower

HEUCHERA 'PALACE PURPLE'

This is a robust old favourite with neat dense mounds of evergreen leaves that made it a popular choice for ground cover and edging. Modern hybrids have improved the size and colour range of the tiny bell-shaped flowers, which are now available in colours from white to crimson, in dense clusters that last for many weeks in almost any position.

Flowering time: Early to late summer.

Height: 30–75cm (12–30in)

Spread: 30–45cm (12–18in)

Soil: Any well-drained, fertile soil.

Positioning: Full sun or semi-shade 30cm (12in) apart a ground cover under trees and shrubs, beside paths, at the front of borders.

Care: Plant in autumn or spring in well-dug so with some compost. Feed with general fertilizer in spring and mulch with compost. Water in dry weathe Cut down stems after flowering; feed agai Divide every 3–4 years.

Propagation: Divide in autumn or spring; sow in a fram in spring.

Recommended: 'Pewter Moon', 'Red Spangles', 'Rachel', 'Snow Storm'.

Useful tip: Plant deeply with crowns at surface lev when roots eventually heave above the surface, earth up or replant in autumn.

Related plants: H. micrantha var. diversifolia 'Palace Purple'; H. cylindrica 'Greenfinch'.

owering time: Early to late summer.

Height: 45–60cm (18–24in).

Spread: 60cm (24in) or more.

Soil: Cool, leafy, moist.

Positioning: Light or semi-shade (full sun if constantly moist); singly or 60cm (2ft) apart, beside trees, shrubs, water features, and as ground cover.

Care: Plant in spring in deeply dug soil with plenty of compost or leaf mould. Protect against slugs. Feed with general fertilizer in spring and mulch with compost or leaf mould. Water in dry weather. Deadhead.

Propagation: Divide in early spring.

ecommended: *H. fortunei*, and *aurea*, var. *albopicta*, var. *aureomarginata*, var. *hyacinthina*; *H. sieboldiana*, and var. *elegans*; *H. ventricosa*.

Useful tip: Plants improve with age so do not disturb without good cause.

Related plants: Many fine hybrids including 'Blue Angel', 'Frances Rivers', 'Honey Bells', 'Krossa Regal', 'Royal Standard', 'Thomas Hogg', 'Wide Brim'.

HOSTA VAR. ALBOPICTA

Both the tall hyacinth-like blooms and dramatically coloured leaves of these supreme foliage plants are coveted for indoor arrangements. In the garden, plants mature into broad leafy clumps that make striking highlights and very effective ground cover for shady borders.

INULA HOOKERI

Plants are large and ornamental, often with huge leaves; the bright yellow blooms are equally bold and quite distinctive with their numerous fine, almost thread-like petals. Deep fertile soil is essential for this stout and enduring perennial, which adapts to most conditions but is particularly happy on shaded clay.

Flowering time: Early summer to early autumn.

Height: Up to 90cm (3ft).

Spread: 60–75cm (2–2½ft).

Soil: Any moist (but not waterlogged) soil.

Positioning: Full sun or semi-shade; singly or 45cm (18in) apart in borders or wild gardens.

Care: Plant in autumn or spring in deeply dug soil with plenty of compost. Feed with general fertilizer in spring and mulch thickly with compost. Water regularly in dry weather. Cut down stems after flowering. Divide every 3 years.

Propagation: Divide in early spring; sow in a frame in spring.

Recommended: *I. ensifolia*, and dwarf 'Compacta', 'Gold Star'; *Inula helenium* for herb gardens; *I. hookeri*; *I. royleana*; *I. magnifica*, 1.2m (6ft) tall, wild gardens.

Useful tip: Roots run very deep: before planting prepare the soil very thoroughly.

Related plants: *Inula* 'Golden Beauty', now *Buphthalmum salicifolium*.

Flowering time:	Late spring and early summer.
Height:	23–90cm (9in–3ft).
Spread:	Up to 45cm (18in).
Soil:	Any well-drained soil (not acid).
Positioning:	Full sun; 30cm (12in) apart in borders and special beds; dwarf kinds in rock gardens.
Care:	Plant in late summer in well-dug soil with some compost and bonemeal, and lime if acid. Bury rhizomes to half their depth, or completely cover in sandy soil, and trim top half of leaves. Feed with general fertilizer in spring and after flowering. Deadhead. Divide crowded rhizomes.
Propagation:	Divide after flowering; replant young portions with 1–2 leaf fans.
Recommended:	Dwarf: 'Blue Doll', 'Gingerbread Man'. Intermediate: 'Curlew', 'Ruby Chimes'. Tall: 'Dancer's Veil', 'Jane Phillips', 'Top Flight'.
Useful tip:	In windy positions, shorten leaves by half in mid-autumn.
Related plants:	*I. unguicularis* and *I. sibirica* varieties.

IRIS 'IMPETUOUS'

Bearded irises make a fine display grown together in a dedicated bed, and there are several hundred flamboyant varieties to choose from in specialist lists. They are undemanding plants if given sun and good drainage, and soon multiply into dense clumps. (syns *I. barbata*, *I. germanica*.)

KNIPHOFIA 'ATLANTA'

Cream, yellow, orange and red are all found in modern red hot pokers, as single colours or with flowers distinctively tipped in a contrasting shade. Leave plants undisturbed to increase in size, but protect them in cold winters as some of the choicest kinds are slightly tender. (syn. *Tritoma*.)

Flowering time:	Late spring to early autumn, according to variety.
Height:	Up to 1.2m (4ft).
Spread:	90cm (3ft).
Soil:	Any well-drained soil.
Positioning:	Full sun or very light shade; singly or 75cm (30in) apart, in mid-border or massed in isolation.
Care:	Plant in autumn or spring in deeply dug soil with added bonemeal. Mulch in spring with compost. Feed with general fertilizer after flowering. Water in dry weather. Leave foliage over winter for protection; tidy in spring.
Propagation:	Divide in spring; sow in a frame in mid-spring.
Recommended:	'Atlanta', 'Border Ballet', 'Little Maid', 'Early Buttercup', 'Prince Igor', 'Royal Standard', 'Tuckii'.
Useful tip:	Leaves have sharp edges, so wear gloves when handling plants.
Related plants:	Peach-white *K. caulescens*; grass-like *K. galpinii*, *K. triangularis*.

Lamium maculatum (Spotted) Dead Nettle

Flowering time: Mid-summer to early autumn.

Height: 20cm (8in).

Spread: 60–75cm (24–30in).

Soil: Any moist, fertile soil.

Positioning: Full sun or shade (best in semi-shade); singly or 38–45cm (15–18in) apart, at the front of borders, as ground cover among shrubs.

Care: Plant any time from early autumn to late spring in lightly dug soil with some compost. Feed with general fertilizer in spring. Water in dry weather. Cut back exhausted stems after flowering; trim when growth is untidy.

Propagation: Divide in autumn or spring.

Recommended: Many good forms, especially *album*, 'Aureum' (syn. 'Gold Leaf'), 'Beacon Silver', 'Chequers', 'Pink Pewter', 'White Nancy'.

Useful tip: Plant among hostas and other shade-loving perennials.

Related plants: *L. galeobdolon* (Yellow Archangel) 'Hermann's Pride', 'Florentinum'.

LAMIUM MACULATUM ALBUM

Lamiums have creeping runners which spread quickly when plants are happy, and are regarded by some gardeners as the perfect ground cover plant, by others as an invasive menace. They soon deteriorate in very dry conditions. Keep moist and shaded to enhance the leaf colouring of the best forms.

Leucanthemum × superbum Shasta Daisy

LEUCANTHEMUM × SUPERBUM

Most old gardens have at least one example of Shasta daisy, a plant that survives neglect but repays a little care with a great flourish of large white or yellow blooms, up to 10cm (4in) across and often fully double. It is an excellent plant both for garden use and as a cut flower. (syns *Chrysanthemum maximum*, *C. × superbum*.)

Flowering time: Early to late summer.
Height: Up to 90cm (3ft).
Spread: 45–60cm (18–24in).
Soil: Moist, fertile.
Positioning: Full sun or very light shade; 38–45cm (15–18in) apart in small groups in the front and middle of borders.
Care: Plant in spring in well-dug soil with plenty of compost, and lime if acid. Feed in late spring with general fertilizer, mulch with compost; water thoroughly in dry weather. Deadhead. Cut down to ground level in late autumn. Divide every 3 years.
Propagation: Divide in spring; grow cuttings in a frame in spring.
Recommended: 'Aglaia', 'Bishopstone' 'Esther Read', 'Phyllis Smith', 'Snowcap', 'Wirral Supreme'.
Useful tip: Plants that are cut back, fed and watered regularly after flowering often bloom again in autumn.
Related plants: *L. vulgare* (Ox-eye Daisy), and 'Maikönigin' (syn. 'May Queen').

Flowering time: Early summer to early autumn.

Height: Up to 1.8m (6ft), usually less.

Spread: 90cm (3ft).

Soil: Rich, consistently moist.

Positioning: Light or semi-shade; singly or 60–75cm (2–2½ft) apart in groups, in shady borders, wild gardens, beside water.

Care: Plant in spring in well-dug soil with plenty of compost or decayed manure. Feed in spring with general fertilizer; mulch lavishly with compost or decayed manure. Water well in dry weather. Cut back stems after flowering, all growth in late autumn. Divide every 3–4 years.

Propagation: Divide in spring; sow in a frame in spring.

Recommended: L. dentata (syn. L. clivorum) and 'Desdemona', 'Orange Princess'; L. × hessei.

Useful tip: Watch out for slugs attacking young leaves.

Related plants: Fine Ligularia hybrids include 'Gregynog Gold', 'The Rocket', 'Weihenstephan'.

LIGULARIA PRZEWALSKII 'THE ROCKET'

Ligularia is a majestic plant, with heart-shaped leaves often 30cm (12in) or more across, and imposing stems which bear a few very large yellow or orange daisies, or masses of smaller ones according to variety. It needs plenty of room, and soil as moist as a bog garden if it is to reach its full potential.

Liriope muscari Lily Turf

LIRIOPE MUSCARI

This is one of those invaluable easy-going plants that gardeners take for granted. It will grow virtually anywhere except on very chalky soils, remains evergreen in most districts and is regularly covered all autumn with spikes of bell-shaped flowers like those of grape hyacinths.

Flowering time: Late summer to late autumn.

Height: 30–45cm (12–18in).

Spread: 30–38cm (12–15in).

Soil: Fertile, well-drained (not too chalky).

Positioning: Full sun or semi-shade; 30cm (12in) apart in drifts at the front of borders, among shrubs.

Care: Plant in autumn or spring in lightly dug soil with a little compost or bonemeal. Feed with general fertilizer in spring. Water now and then on very dry soils. Cut down stems after flowering; tidy foliage in spring.

Propagation: Divide in spring; sow in a frame or in situ in spring.

Recommended: Basic species and 'Majestic', 'Monroe White' (syn. *alba*), 'Royal Purple', 'Superba'; variegated 'Gold-banded'.

Useful tip: Divide only when clumps become congested or invasive, or fail to flower.

Related plants: *L. spicata* (Creeping Lily Turf), and 'Alba', 'Silver Dragon'.

Flowering time:	Early and mid-summer, often again in early autumn.
Height:	Up to 1.2m (4ft).
Spread:	60–90cm (2–3ft).
Soil:	Any well-drained soil, with little or no lime.
Positioning:	Full sun or very light shade; singly or 60cm (2ft) apart in borders.
Care:	Plant in autumn or spring in well-dug soil with added bonemeal. Feed with general fertilizer in spring and immediately after flowering. Protect against slugs. Support in exposed gardens. Cut to ground level in late autumn; cover with leaves in cold areas. Spray with aphids.
Propagation:	Grow cuttings under glass in spring; sow in a frame in spring.
Recommended:	'Ann Gregg', 'Band of Nobles', 'Chandelier', 'My Castle', 'Noble Maiden', 'The Page', 'Troop the Colour'.
Useful tip:	For further blooms, prune stems hard after flowering, and feed.
Related plants:	L. arboreus (Tree Lupin), and 'Golden Spire', 'Mauve Queen'.

LUPIN POLYPHYLLUS

There are dozens of gorgeous hybrids, with more appearing every year. All are adaptable and relatively easy to grow, if you accept that they are short-lived and prefer slightly acid conditions with little humus. Plant a rich mixture and save the seeds – many seedlings will be as glorious as their parents.

LYCHNIS CHALCEDONICA

This is perhaps the best known member of the varied Lychnis or catchfly family, and is certainly the most fiery. The heads of scarlet long-lasting blooms crown tall stems which, if cut back after flowering, will branch and produce a small later crop. A combination of red, pink and white forms makes a startling display.

Flowering time: Early to late summer.
Height: 90cm (3ft).
Spread: 30–45cm (12–18in)
Soil: Any well-drained soil.
Positioning: Full sun; 45cm (18in) apart in bold groups mid-border, in front of evergreen shrubs.
Care: Plant in spring in lightly dug soil with a little compost. Feed with general fertilizer in spring. Water well in dry weather. Support flower stems in exposed positions. Deadhead; cut all growth to the ground late autumn.
Propagation: Divide in spring; sow in a frame in spring.
Recommended: Basic species and 'Alba' (white), double 'Flore Pleno', pink 'Carnea', 'Rosea' and 'Rosea Plena'.
Useful tip: The basic colour is vivid, so position plant carefully against other flowers.
Related plants: L. × arkwrightii and 'Vesuvius'; L. coronaria (Rose Campion); L. flos-cuculi 'Nana', dwarf Ragged Robin; L. viscaria (Catchfly), especially double 'Splendens Plena'.

owering time: Early summer to early autumn.

Height: 30–60cm (1–2ft).

Spread: 30cm (1ft).

Soil: Dry, well-drained.

Positioning: Best in shade of all kinds (but tolerates full sun); 23–30cm (9–12in) apart in patches in shrubberies, borders, as edging.

Care: Plant in autumn or spring in well-dug soil with added compost and bonemeal. Feed in spring with general fertilizer. Water freely in very dry weather. Deadhead to prevent excessive seeding. Cut to ground level in mid-autumn.

Propagation: Sow in situ in autumn.

commended: Basic species and double *flore-pleno*, var. *aurantiaca* (orange), 'Frances Perry' (scarlet).

Useful tip: Self-sown seedlings are best transplanted while still very small.

elated plants: *M. × sheldonii*, and Crewdson Hybrids, 'Slieve Donard' – easier than blue forms like *M. betonicifolia*, syn. *M. baileyi* (Blue Tibetan Poppy).

MECONOPSIS CAMBRICA

This is an enchanting poppy and certainly the least demanding *Meconopsis*, most species of which need careful siting and usually die after flowering. Welsh poppies will grow almost anywhere, but spread fastest in dry shade where they mingle with other plants and soon build colonies that are easy to control.

Monarda hybrids Bergamot, Bee Balm, Oswego Tea

MONARDA 'CROFTWAY PINK'

Many lovely colours have been introduced into the modern hybrids of this familiar cottage and herb garden plant. Plants are strong and bushy, and all parts are highly aromatic with citrus overtones; the spectacular flowers are extremely popular with bees – and with flower arrangers.

Flowering time: Early summer to early autumn.
Height: 90cm (3ft).
Spread: 30–45cm (12–18in).
Soil: Rich, moist.
Positioning: Full sun or very light shade; 23–30cm (9–12in) apart in bold groups in mid-border, beside water, in herb gardens.
Care: Plant in autumn or spring in well-dug soil with plenty of compost or decayed manure. Feed in spring with general fertilizer and mulch with compost o decayed manure. Water freely in dry weather. In autumn cu stems to ground level and mulch on light soils. Divide every 2–4 years.
Propagation: Divide in spring; sow in a frame in spring.
Recommended: 'Beauty of Cobham', 'Schneewittchen' (syn. 'Snow White'), 'Squaw', 'Panorama'.
Useful tip: Watch out for mildew in late summer.
Related plants: *M. didyma* and white 'Alba', herb garden plants; *M. fistulosa* (Wild Bergamot) tolerates drought.

Nepeta × faassenii (Blue) Catmint

Flowering time: Late spring to early autumn.

Height: 60cm (2ft).

Spread: 38–45cm (15–18in).

Soil: Any fertile, well-drained soil.

Positioning: Full sun or very light shade; 30cm (12in) apart as edging and ground cover in borders, herb gardens, rose beds.

Care: Plant in autumn or spring in lightly dug soil with added bonemeal, and grit in heavy soils. Feed with general fertilizer in spring; mulch with compost or leaf mould in autumn. Cut down foliage at the end of winter.

Propagation: Divide in autumn (light soil only) or spring.

Recommended: Basic species; also hybrids 'Six Hills Giant', 'Thornbury'.

Useful tip: Support tall varieties with peasticks or trim straggling stems occasionally.

Related plants: N. cataria 'Citriodora'; dwarf N. nervosa; N. sibirica 'Souvenir d'André Chaudron' (syn. N. 'Blue Beauty').

NEPETA × FAASSENII

Catmints are popular aromatic edging plants that seem to be in full bloom for most of the summer, and survive for many years in well-drained soil; only winter dampness discourages this attractive plant. There are several kinds that look very similar, and many gardens have unidentified examples.

OENOTHERA MACROCARPA

As the name suggests, the flowers of the evening primrose first open as the sun begins to sink, when the pointed buds, often rich red in colour, expand into papery yellow, white or pink blooms up to 8cm (3in) across. Good drainage is far more important than fertility for success with these plants.

Flowering time:	Early summer to early autumn.
Height:	Short: 30–45cm (12–18in). Tall: up to 1.5m (5ft).
Spread:	30–45cm (12–18in).
Soil:	Any well-drained soil.
Positioning:	Full sun; 30cm (12in) apart in groups in borders, rockeries, wild gardens.
Care:	Plant in spring in well-dug soil with added bonemeal. Feed with general fertilizer in late spring, and mulch with compost or leaf mould. Water in dry weather. Support tall varieties in exposed positions. Cut stems to ground level in late autumn.
Propagation:	Divide in spring; grow cuttings in a frame in late spring; sow under glass in spring.
Recommended:	O. fruticosa and 'Fireworks'; O. macrocarpa (syn. O. missouriensis).
Useful tip:	Plants are also effective dispersed singly among other perennials.
Related plants:	O. acaulis 'Aurea' and O. speciosa, sometimes treated as biennials.

lowering time: Late spring and early summer.

Height: 45–90cm (1½–3ft).

Spread: 45–75cm (18–30in).

Soil: Any deep, rich soil.

Positioning: Full sun or very light shade; singly or 60cm (2ft) apart in groups of 3, in borders, near the front of shrubberies.

Care: Plant in early autumn, 2.5–5cm (1–2in) deep in well-dug soil with plenty of compost or decayed manure. Feed with general fertilizer in spring and after flowering. Water in dry weather. Support lax stems. Mulch in autumn with decayed manure or compost. Leave foliage to protect crowns in winter.

Propagation: Divide tuberous roots in spring; sow in a frame in spring.

Recommended: *P. lactiflora* hybrids 'Festiva Maxima', 'Karl Rosenfield', 'Monsieur Jules Elie'.

Useful tip: The red young foliage contrasts dramatically with forget-me-nots.

Related plants: *P. officinalis* hybrids like 'China Rose' and *P. mlokosewitschii* flower very early.

PAEONIA 'CHINA ROSE'

A peony is a long-term investment which will flower for 50 years or more if happy, so good preparation is worthwhile. The plants enjoy rich living, and in return provide a lavish display of opulent blooms, sometimes 15cm (6in) or more across, in a wide array of colours and complex forms.

PAPAVER ORIENTALE 'CURLILOCKS'

A packet of mixed seeds will supply a fine range of colours to grace any border, but for supreme quality and beauty named hybrids must be grown. Plants live for many years and increase in size and impact. The spectacular flowers last well in vases if they are cut just before the buds burst fully open.

Flowering time: Late spring to mid-summer.

Height: 60–90cm (2–3ft).

Spread: Up to 90cm (3ft).

Soil: Any deep, well-drained soil.

Positioning: Full sun or very light shade; singly or 45cm (18in) apart, in the front or middle of borders, beside water.

Care: Plant in autumn or spring in deeply dug soil with added bonemeal. Feed with general fertilizer in spring and after flowering; mulch lavishly with compost in autumn. Support sprawling stems with peasticks.

Propagation: Divide in spring or late summer; sow in a frame in spring.

Recommended: Many hybrids including 'Allegro', 'Black and White', 'Marcus Perry', 'Mrs Perry', 'Picotée'.

Useful tip: Grow beside mid-summer perennials for colour when the poppies die down.

Related plants: 'Pizzicato', mixture of very dwarf hybrids easily raised from seed.

lowering time: Early summer to early autumn.

Height: 45–75cm (18–30in).

Spread: 38–45cm (15–18in).

Soil: Dry, very well-drained.

Positioning: Full sun or very light shade, sheltered from hard frost; singly or 38cm (15in) apart in groups in mid-border.

Care: Plant in spring in deeply dug soil with some compost. Feed with general fertilizer in spring and mid-summer. Water in dry weather. Support in exposed positions. Cut down in autumn, and mulch with compost or leaf mould.

Propagation: Grow cuttings in a frame in summer; sow under glass in early spring.

Recommended: 'Alice Hindley', 'Apple Blossom', 'Burgundy', 'Evelyn', 'Hidcote Pink', 'Schoenholzeri', 'King George'.

Useful tip: In cold gardens, take cuttings in summer and overwinter in a frame. Treat plants as annuals.

Related plants: P. hirsutus 'Pygmaeus', P. newberryi, rock garden miniatures.

PENSTEMON 'SOUR GRAPES'

These glorious plants are very popular despite the difficulty of keeping them through a hard winter. Severe frost can be lethal, especially if the soil is wet in winter, but plants are easily propagated from cuttings, a method recommended as an annual insurance in most gardens.

PHLOX PANICULATA HYBRID

Perennial borders are incomplete without phlox hybrids and their brilliant late summer colour, massed in single or mixed shades. There are dozens of forms, most of them very fragrant. Their flowers, held in impressively large and long-lasting trusses, range from deep purple to white.

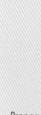

Flowering time:	Mid-summer to mid-autumn.
Height:	Up to 1.2m (4ft).
Spread:	45–60cm (18–24in).
Soil:	Rich, moist.
Positioning:	Full sun or light shade 45cm (18in) apart, massed in mid-border.
Care:	Plant in autumn or spring in deeply dug soil with plenty of compost or decayed manure. Feed with general fertilizer in spring and mid-summer; mulch with compost or decayed manure in autumn; water in dry weather. Cut down almost to ground level in late autumn.
Propagation:	Divide in autumn or spring.
Recommended:	'Amethyst', 'Brigadier' 'Eventide', 'Fujiyama', 'Prince of Orange', 'Star Fire'.
Useful tip:	Stunted shoots, narrow foliage indicate stem eel worm. Do *not* divide: take root cuttings and grow in fresh soil.
Related plants:	*P. maculata,* and 'Alpha', 'Omega'; *P. stolonifera,* hybrids for edging rockeries.

Flowering time: Mid-summer to early autumn.

Height: 90cm–1.2m (3–4ft).

Spread: 38–45cm (15–18in).

Soil: Any deep soil.

Positioning: Full sun or semi-shade; 45cm (18in) apart in groups in the middle or back of borders, and as isolated highlights.

Care: Plant in autumn or spring in deeply dug soil with plenty of compost. Feed with general fertilizer in spring and when flowering starts; mulch light soils with grass clippings in spring. Water in dry weather. Tall varieties may need support. Cut down stems in autumn. Divide every 5 years.

Propagation: Divide in spring; sow under glass in spring.

Recommended: Basic species and 'Alba' (white), 'Vivid', 'Bouquet Rose', 'Rosea', 'Summer Snow', 'Variegata'.

Useful tip: Grow in light shade for the best colours and extended flowering.

Related plants: 'Rose Crown', 'Crown of Snow', good seed strains.

PHYSOSTEGIA VIRGINIANA 'VIVID'

Bend the tubular flowers of this fascinating old-fashioned cottage garden plant and they will remain in that position, for each is attached to the stem by a flexible joint. It adapts to almost any condition and is a sound choice for difficult soils and aspects. (syn. *Dracocephalum virginianum*.)

63

POLEMONIUM FOLIOSISSIMUM

The common name of this well-loved perennial reflects the shape of the pretty foliage, which is divided into several successive pairs of leaflets like the rungs of a ladder. Blue, pink and white forms are available, and are all very striking when grown *en masse*.

Flowering time: Late spring to mid-summer.

Height: 45–90cm (1½–3ft).

Spread: 30–60cm (1–2ft).

Soil: Any fertile soil.

Positioning: Full sun or shade; singly or 30–45cm (12–18in) apart in natural patches, in mi border, wild gardens wooded corners.

Care: Plant in autumn or spring in lightly forked soil with some compost. In spring fee with general fertilizer, mulch with compost o light soils. Water in very dry weather. Support tall forms. Cu to ground level in autumn.

Propagation: Divide in autumn or spring; sow under glass in mid-spring.

Recommended: *P. caeruleum*, and *album* (white), 'Blue Bell', 'Hopleys'; also *P.* 'Lambrook Mauve', *P.* 'Sapphire'.

Useful tip: Deadhead plants regularly to extend flowering throughout the summer.

Related plants: *P. carneum* 'Apricot Beauty'; *P. reptans* 'Blue Pearl'; *P. foliosissimum*.

Flowering time: Mid-spring to early summer.

Height: Up to 1.2m (4ft).

Spread: 60–75cm (2–2½ft).

Soil: Rich, moist.

Positioning: Cool shade or semi-shade; 60cm (2ft) apart in groups under trees and in other positions that are not hot and dry.

Care: Plant early in autumn or spring in deeply dug soil with plenty of compost or leaf mould: Set the rhizomes just below ground level. Feed with general fertilizer in spring and as flowers fade. Water in dry weather. Cut down stems in autumn. Watch out for sawfly caterpillars in summer.

Propagation: Divide after flowering; sow in a frame in autumn.

Recommended: Basic species and double 'Flore Pleno', variegated 'Striatum'.

Useful tip: Combine with ferns and hostas to create a natural woodland partnership.

Related plants: Fragrant P. odoratum 'Variegatum', 'Flore Pleno'; P. hookeri, lilac flowers.

POLYGONATUM × HYBRIDUM

Woodland shade characterizes the native habitat of this unusual plant, which has thick creeping rhizomes that wander far in moist soil. Its tall elegant stems are decked with leaves and hanging clusters of green-tipped white bells. Allow plants plenty of room and then leave them to multiply into large leafy masses. (syn. *P. multiflorum*.)

Pulsatilla Pasque Flower

PULSATILLA PATENS

Fat woolly buds first appear in early spring, and open into deep colourful goblets, 8cm (3in) across, against a background of soft ferny leaves which persist all season. Finally the flowering stems, by now twice their original height, produce decorative silky seedheads filled with masses of viable seeds.

Flowering time: Early and mid-spring.
Height: 20–30cm (8–12in).
Spread: 30–38cm (12–15in).
Soil: Dryish, well-drained, preferably chalk.
Positioning: Full sun or very light shade; 30cm (12in) apart in large isolated groups and at the front of borders.
Care: Plant firmly in autumn or spring in well-dug soil with added grit for drainage. Feed with general fertilizer after flowering. Water in a dry summer.
Propagation: Sow in a frame in autumn and expose to cold.
Recommended: *P. vulgaris* and *alba* (white), 'Flore Pleno', 'Eva Constance', 'Röde Klokke', *rubra*, 'White Swan'.
Useful tip: Plants are also suitable for rock gardens and containers, and are especially effective when they are given a gravel mulch.
Related plants: *P. alpina* (white) and ssp. *apiifolia*, syn. *Anemone sulfurea* (yellow), silver seedheads; *P. patens* (Eastern Pasque Flower), very hardy.

owering time: Mid-summer to mid-autumn.

Height: 60–90cm (2–3ft).

Spread: 45–60cm (18–24in).

Soil: Any fertile, well-drained soil.

Positioning: Full sun or semi-shade; 45cm (18in) apart in groups in mid-border or massed in isolation.

Care: Plant in autumn or spring in deeply dug soil with plenty of compost. Feed with general fertilizer in spring and when flowering starts; mulch light soils with compost in late spring. Support taller varieties. Deadhead regularly. Cut to ground level in late autumn.

Propagation: Divide in autumn or spring; sow in a frame in spring.

ecommended: Var. *deamii*, var. *speciosa*, var. *sullivantii* 'Goldsturm'.

Useful tip: In fertile soil divide plants every 3–5 years to keep them under control.

elated plants: Other good rudbeckias include 'Goldquelle', 'Herbstsonne', 'Juligold'.

RUDBECKIA VAR. SULLIVANTII 'GOLDSTURM'

The old-fashioned tall rudbeckias are invasive and best avoided in favour of shorter bushy hybrids. These produce masses of bright yellow, gold or orange daisies, up to 13cm (5in) across with prominent dark centres, that are stunning when massed in large patches and excellent as cut flowers.

Flowering time: Mid-summer to early autumn.

Height: 60–90cm (2–3ft).

Spread: 38–45cm (15–18in).

Soil: Any well-drained soil.

Positioning: Full sun or very light shade; 38cm (15in) apart in groups in mid border, against a warm wall, beside water.

Care: Plant in autumn or spring in deeply dug soil with some bonemeal. Feed with general fertilizer in early spring. Water until established. Support tall stems in exposed positions. Deadhead.

Propagation: Divide in autumn or spring; grow cuttings under glass in late spring.

Recommended: Basic species and 'Rubin', 'Superba'.

Useful tip: Overfeeding produces lush leaves at the expense of blooms.

Related plants: Other attractive forms include S. nemorosa 'East Friesland', 'Rose Queen'; S. × sylvestris 'Blue Queen', 'May Knight', 'Rose Queen'; S. uliginosa.

SALVIA × SUPERBA

There are many handsome sages that make a strong impression in perennial borders, although some are difficult to keep in less than ideal conditions. This species is one of the more reliable, with strong upright growth and tall slender spikes of blue, pink or purple flowers that persist for many weeks.

Saxifraga umbrosa
Porcelain Flower, London Pride

lowering time: Late spring to mid-summer.

Height: 30cm (12in).

Spread: 45–60cm (18–24in).

Soil: Any moist soil.

Positioning: Light or semi-shade; 45cm (18in) apart as ground cover, edging and specimen groups in rock gardens, at the front of borders.

Care: Plant in spring in well-dug soil with some compost or leaf mould, and mulch heavy soils with grit for good drainage. Feed with general fertilizer in spring. Deadhead.

Propagation: Separate rosettes in spring; sow in a frame in spring.

Recommended: Basic species and dwarf var. *primuloides*, fine gold-marked form *variegata* (now S. 'Aureopunctata'); S. × *urbium* (London Pride).

Useful tip: Plants can tolerate full sun, and in northern districts this is essential for healthy growth.

Related plants: S. 'Clarence Elliott' (syn. S. *umbrosa* var. *primuloides* 'Elliott's Variety'), deep pink, compact.

SAXIFRAGA UMBROSA

There can be few old gardens without an example, if not a whole edging strip, of London pride, strictly a hybrid of this species and perhaps the best-known saxifrage. Plants withstand pollution and will grow in the most inhospitable places, with neat dense growth all year.

69

SCABIOSA CAUCASICA 'STÄFA'

The basic species of this late perennial, immensely popular for cutting, has lilac-blue or frilled white flowers, but hybrids have extended the colour range through the whole blue spectrum. Plants are long-lived on chalky soils, much less so on acid ones unless lime is added at planting time.

Flowering time:	Early summer to early or mid-autumn.
Height:	45–60cm (18–24in).
Spread:	60cm (24in).
Soil:	Any well-drained soil.
Positioning:	Full sun; 45cm (18in) apart in natural patches at the front of borders, beside paths.
Care:	Plant in spring, fairly deeply in well-dug soil with plenty of compost or leaf mould, and lime in acid soils. Feed with general fertilizer in spring; mulch in early summer with grass clippings. Deadhead regularly; cut to ground level in late autumn. Divide every 3 years.
Propagation:	Divide in spring; sow in a frame in spring.
Recommended:	Basic species and varieties like *alba*, 'Clive Greaves', 'Fama', 'Miss Willmott', 'Moerheim Blue'; *S. columbaria* 'Butterfly Blue'.
Useful tip:	Harvest the blooms freely for arranging in vases, as cutting them prolongs flowering.
Related plants:	Good seed mixtures include Dwarf Double Hybrids, Giant Imperial.

lowering time: Early autumn or early winter.

Height: Up to 60cm (2ft).

Spread: 23–30cm (9–12in).

Soil: Moist, fertile.

Positioning: Full sun, sheltered from cold winds and hard frost; 25cm (10in) apart in natural groups in any very moist position.

Care: Plant in spring, in deeply dug soil with plenty of compost or leaf mould. Feed with general fertilizer in spring. Water in dry weather. Cut down stems in early winter and mulch with compost or leaf mould.

Propagation: Divide or separate young offshoots in spring; replant immediately.

Recommended: Basic species and hybrids like *alba* (white), 'Jennifer', 'Major', 'Mrs Hegarty', 'November Cheer', 'Professor Barnard', 'Sunrise'.

Useful tip: Grow plants near water if possible: moist air is said to improve flowering.

Related plants: *Crocosmia masoniorum.*

SCHIZOSTYLIS COCCINEA

A lot of moisture is essential for these plants to flower well, and they are most successful in a bog garden. Blooms appear very late and the lilies prefer a warm sheltered position. Although sold as bulbs, plants are strictly perennials with rhizomatous roots.

SEDUM SPECTABILE 'BRILLIANT'

Late butterflies depend on the flat 15cm (6in) flower heads of sedums such as this for browsing in autumn. The plants are tough, thriving in very spartan conditions, and form compact clusters for most of the season until the flower stems begin to extend towards the end of summer. (syn. *Hylotelephium spectabile*.)

Flowering time:	Late summer to mid-autumn.
Height:	Up to 50cm (20in).
Spread:	45cm (18in).
Soil:	Light, dry, well-drained.
Positioning:	Full sun; 30cm (12in) apart in informal groups, as edging for paths and borders, and in larger rock gardens.
Care:	Plant in autumn or spring in well-dug soil with added bonemeal and grit on heavy soil. Feed with organic slow-release fertilizer in late spring. Cut down flower stems in early winter; trim plants to size in spring.
Propagation:	Divide in autumn or spring; sow in a frame in spring.
Recommended:	Basic species and 'Brilliant', 'Meteor', 'Stardust' ('Variegatum' is now *S. alboroseum* 'Mediovariegatum').
Useful tip:	Plants thrive on thin dry soils, and do not respond well to ordinary fertilizers.
Related plants:	*S. spurium* hybrids, and 'Schorbuser Blut' (syn. 'Dragon's Blood').

Flowering time: Early summer to early autumn.

Height: 60cm–1.2m (2–4ft).

Spread: 45cm (18in).

Soil: Any fertile soil.

Positioning: Full sun or semi-shade, sheltered from strong winds; 30–38cm (12–15in) apart in groups in mid-border.

Care: Plant in spring in well-dug soil with a little compost. Feed with general fertilizer in spring and at the start of flowering, and mulch with compost on very dry ground. Water in dry weather. Support tall varieties; cut down stems immediately after flowering. In cold gardens, mulch in early winter with dry leaves or leaf mould.

Propagation: Divide in spring; sow in a frame in spring.

Recommended: 'Croftway Red', 'Elsie Heugh', 'Loveliness', 'Party Girl', 'Rose Queen', 'William Smith'; seed mixtures like 'Stark's Hybrids'.

Useful tip: Avoid disturbing established plants.

Related plants: S. candida (White Prairie Mallow).

SIDALCEA 'LOVELINESS'

Flowering plants resemble small hollyhocks (in the USA the common name is wild hollyhock), and freely bear 2.5cm (1in) blooms on tall slender spikes that last for weeks in water. Plants improve in size and quality as the years pass, provided fertility levels are kept high.

SISYRINCHIUM STRIATUM

Flowering time:	Early to late summer.
Height:	30–60cm (1–2ft).
Spread:	Up to 60cm (2ft).
Soil:	Light, dry, well-drained.
Positioning:	Full sun; 30cm (12in) apart in small groups beside paths, in gravel areas, at the front of dry borders, in joints in paving, patios.
Care:	Plant in spring in well-dug soil with added compost, and grit for drainage. Feed with general fertilizer in spring and after flowering. Water when weather is very dry. Deadhead.
Propagation:	Remove rooted offshoots in late summer; sow in a frame in spring.
Recommended:	Basic species and variegated 'Aunt May' (syn. *variegatum*), 'Rushfields'.
Useful tip:	Do not disturb unnecessarily; a hard winter may injure the leaves, but plants recover quickly.
Related plants:	Most other species are dwarf rock garden plants; some are now called *Gelasine* or *Olsynium*.

This species is the giant of the Sisyrinchium family, much taller than others and with more prominent flower stems. The stems grow as extensions of the leaves and die after flowering, so care with feeding is important to ensure clumps do not flower themselves to death. Contented plants may become invasive, but seedlings are easily transplanted.

Stachys byzantina Lamb's Ears, Lamb's Tongue

Flowering time: Early to late summer.
Height: 38–60cm (15–24in).
Spread: 30–38cm (12–15in).
Soil: Dry, well-drained.
Positioning: Full sun or semi-shade; singly or 30cm (12in) apart in small groups, as edging, ground cover.
Care: Plant in autumn or spring in deeply dug soil with a little compost, and grit if soil is heavy. Feed in spring with high-potash fertilizer. Cut off flower stems if grown as foliage plants. Cut back in autumn. Mulch with grit in autumn to prevent leaves rotting on wet soil.
Propagation: Divide in autumn or spring.
Recommended: Basic species and 'Big Ears', 'Primrose Heron', 'Silver Carpet', variegated 'Striped Phantom'.
Useful tip: This makes attractive ground cover under old-fashioned roses.
Related plants: S. macrantha (syn. S. grandiflora), Betonica macrantha (Big Betony), and 'Robusta', 'Rosea'.

STACHYS BYZANTINA 'SILVER CARPET'

The large evergreen rosettes of this species are a popular edging for beds and paths, their dense woolly leaves making a handsome carpet of silvery-white all year. The mauve flower spikes are attractive, too, but are often removed to maintain the uniform ground cover. (syns *S. lanata*, *S. olympica*.)

Tellima grandiflora Fringe Cups

TELLIMA GRANDIFLORA

This is chiefly grown as a rapidly spreading ground-cover plant, which produces dense carpets of foliage that effectively suppress weeds. For a few weeks in late spring, however, the evergreen plants bear dainty sprays of tiny flowers, at first greenish but later turning red; pink and pure white forms are also available.

Flowering time:	Late spring and early summer.
Height:	45–60cm (18–24in).
Spread:	45–60cm (18–24in).
Soil:	Any very well-drained soil.
Positioning:	Full sun or semi-shade; 30cm (12in) apart as ground cover, edging to paths or borders, under shrubs and trees.
Care:	Plant in autumn or spring in lightly forked soil with plenty of compost or leaf mould. Feed with general fertilizer in spring. Water until established. Cut down stems after flowering and mulch with compost.
Propagation:	Divide in autumn or spring; sow under glass in spring.
Recommended:	Basic species and white Alba Group, fragrant Odorata Group, red-flushed Rubra Group; also 'Purpurea'.
Useful tip:	Scented blooms of the Odorata Group make charming sprays for small vases.
Related plants:	Several other *Tellima* species are now *Lithophragma*.

Thalictrum delavayi Meadow Rue

lowering time: Early to late summer.

Height: Up to 1.8m (6ft).

Spread: 45–60cm (18–24in).

Soil: Moist, fertile.

Positioning: Full sun to semi-shade; singly or 60cm (2ft) apart, at the back of borders, near trees and tall shrubs, as specimen groups.

Care: Plant in autumn or spring in deeply dug soil with plenty of compost or decayed manure. In spring feed with general fertilizer and mulch with manure. Water in dry weather. Stake in exposed positions. Leave the decorative seedheads until all growth is cut down in late autumn.

Propagation: Divide in autumn or spring; sow in a frame in spring.

Recommended: Basic species and 'Album' (white), 'Hewitt's Double', 'Sternhimmel'.

Useful tip: Plants need 3–4 years to reach full stature.

Related plants: T. aquilegiifolium and purple 'Thundercloud', white 'Album'; dwarf T. minus adiantifolium, dry soils.

THALICTRUM DELAVAYI

Most Thalictrums need moist or even wet soils, and plenty of room for their tall spreading spires of gently nodding flowers. Despite their magnificent stature, plants are light and graceful, with slender stems and ferny leaves that are as popular as the flowers for arrangements. (syn. *T. dipterocarpum*.)

TROLLIUS 'ALABASTER'

These moisture-loving plants resemble superior buttercups, and come from damp meadows or stream margins. They are easy to grow given adequate water, and repay this simple care with a brilliant display of clear yellow, orange or cream flowers 5cm (2in) or more across. (syns *T. × cultorum, T. hybridus.*)

Flowering time: Late spring to mid-summer.

Height: 45–75cm (18–30in).

Spread: 45cm (18in).

Soil: Any moist or wet soil.

Positioning: Full sun to semi-shade; singly or 38–45cm (15–18in) apart in small groups, in bog gardens, borders.

Care: Plant in autumn or spring in deeply dug soil with plenty of compost or leaf mould. Feed with general fertilizer in spring and after flowering; mulch with compost or leaf mould in spring. Water lavishly in dry weather. Cut to ground level in autumn.

Propagation: Divide in autumn or spring; sow under glass in spring.

Recommended: Many good hybrids including 'Alabaster', 'Canary Bird', 'Earliest of All', 'Golden Cup', 'Orange Princess', 'Superbus'.

Useful tip: Trim flower stems when they fade to encourage a second flush.

Related plants: *T. chinensis* (syn. *T. ledebouri*) 'Golden Queen', tall late flowers.

Flowering time:	Late spring to mid-summer.
Height:	Up to 90cm (3ft), often less.
Spread:	30–38cm (12–15in).
Soil:	Any very well-drained soil.
Positioning:	Full sun or very light shade; 30cm (12in) apart in bold groups in mid-border, near water.
Care:	Plant in autumn or spring in deeply dug soil with plenty of compost or leaf mould, and grit on heavy ground. In spring feed with general fertilizer and mulch with compost or leaf mould. Water in dry weather. Cut to ground level in autumn.
Propagation:	Divide in autumn or spring; sow in a frame in spring.
Recommended:	'Ionian Skies', and ssp. *teucrium* forms like 'Kapitän', 'Royal Blue', 'Shirley Blue'.
Useful tip:	Make a feature of the plants' stiff upright habit by massing them as an isolated feature.
Related plants:	*V. spicata* and *V. longifolia* hybrids, later flowering.

VERONICA AUSTRIACA 'CRATER LAKE BLUE'

Speedwell hybrids can supply some of the most intense shades of blue available, and would be indispensable for this quality alone. They have other virtues, though: they are easy to grow, their foliage is semi-evergreen in sheltered spots and their upright habit helps them stand out among other border plants.

VIOLA CORNUTA 'ALBA'

Every border has space for a few sweet violets, which make excellent edging and carpeting under or around other perennials. Their compelling virtues are early flowering, unforgettable fragrance and rapid expansion into large prolific mats, especially on moist fertile soils, supplying numerous cut blooms for posies.

Flowering time:	Early to mid-spring, and again in autumn.
Height:	10–15cm (4–6in).
Spread:	30–38cm (12–15in).
Soil:	Any well-drained, fertile soil.
Positioning:	Full sun to semi-shade (best in light shade); singly or 30cm (12in) apart, as ground cover, edging.
Care:	Plant in autumn in well-dug soil with plenty of compost or decayed manure. Feed with general fertilizer in late winter and after first flowering; mulch with compost or decayed manure in mid-spring. Water in dry weather. Deadhead; trim to shape in autumn. Divide every 3 years.
Propagation:	Divide in autumn; grow cuttings in a frame in summer; sow in a frame in spring.
Recommended:	*V. odorata* and *alba*, 'Amiral Avellan', 'Perle Rose', 'Princess of Wales', 'Rawson's White', 'The Czar'.
Useful tip:	There is confusion between violas, violets and violettas
Related plants:	*V. cornuta* and hybrids; *V.* 'Maggie Mott'.